Contents

4

List of illustrations

BARBARA ADAMS

EGYPTIAN MUMMIES

SHIRE EGYPTOLOGY

Published by
SHIRE PUBLICATIONS LTD.
Cromwell House, Church Street, Princes Risborough,
Aylesbury, Bucks, HP17 9AJ, UK.

Series Editor : Barbara Adams.

British Library Cataloguing in Publication Data
Adams, Barbara
Egyptian mummies — (Shire Egyptology; 1)
1. Mummies
I. Title
393'.3' 0932 DT62.M7

ISBN 0 85263 699 7

First published 1984.

Set in 11 point Times and printed in Great Britain by
C. I. Thomas & Sons (Haverfordwest) Ltd,
Press Buildings, Merlins Bridge, Haverfordwest, Dyfed.

Chronology

From Murnane, W. J. *The Penguin Guide to Ancient Egypt,* 1983.

Predynastic	before 3150 BC	
	3150 - 3050	Late Predynastic - Protodynastic
Early Dynastic	3050 - 2613 BC	
	3050 - 2890	Dynasty I
	2890 - 2686	Dynasty II
	2686 - 2613	Dynasty III
Old Kingdom	2613 - 2181 BC	
	2613 - 2498	Dynasty IV
	2498 - 2345	Dynasty V
	2345 - 2181	Dynasty VI
First Intermediate Period	2181 - 2040 BC	
	2181 - 2040	Dynasties VII-X
	2134 - 2060	Dynasty XI (Theban)
Middle Kingdom	2040 - 1782 BC	
	2060 - 1991	Dynasty XI
	1991 - 1782	Dynasty XII
Second Intermediate Period	1782 - 1570 BC	
	1782 - 1650	Dynasties XIII and XIV (Egyptian)
	1663 - 1555	Dynasties XV and XVI (Hyksos)
	1663 - 1570	Dynasty XVII (Theban)
New Kingdom	1570 - 1070 BC	
	1570 - 1293	*Dynasty XVIII*
	1570 - 1546	Ahmose *
	1551 - 1524	Amenophis I *
	1524 - 1518	Tuthmosis I *
	1518 - 1504	Tuthmosis II *
	1504 - 1450	Tuthmosis III *
	1498 - 1483	Hatshepsut (?)
	1453 - 1419	Amenophis II *
	1419 - 1386	Tuthmosis IV *
	1386 - 1349	Amenophis III *
	1350 - 1334	Amenophis IV/Akhenaten
	1336 - 1334	Smenkhare (?)
	1334 - 1325	Tutankhamun *
	1325 - 1321	Ay
	1321 - 1293	Horemheb
	1293 - 1185	*Dynasty XIX*
	1293 - 1291	Ramesses I
	1291 - 1278	Seti I *
	1279 - 1212	Ramesses II *
	1212 - 1202	Merneptah *
	1202 - 1193	Seti II *
	1193 - 1187	Siptah *
	1187 - 1185	Twosre

* denotes existence of mummy.

	1185 - 1070		*Dynasty XX*
	1185 - 1182		Sethnakhte
	1182 - 1151		Ramesses III *
	1151 - 1145		Ramesses IV *
	1145 - 1141		Ramesses V *
	1141 - 1133		Ramesses VI *
	1133 - 1131		Ramesses VII
	1131 - 1126		Ramesses VIII
	1126 - 1108		Ramesses IX
	1108 - 1098		Ramesses X
	1098 - 1070		Ramesses XI
Third Intermediate Period	1070 - 713 BC		
	1070 -	945	Dynasty XXI
	945 -	712	Dynasty XXII
	828 -	712	Dynasty XXIII
	724 -	713	Dynasty XXIV
Late Period	713 - 332 BC		
	713 -	656	Dynasty XXV (Nubian)
	664 -	525	Dynasty XXVI
	525 -	404	Dynasty XXVII (Persian)
	404 -	399	Dynasty XXVIII
	399 -	380	Dynasty XXIX
	380 -	343	Dynasty XXX (Egyptian/Persian)
Graeco-Roman Period	332 BC to AD 395		
	332 -	30	Ptolemies
	30 BC - AD 395		Roman Emperors

* denotes existence of mummy.

1
Predynastic and Early Dynastic

In a small room, full of fascinating natural material, off the upper gallery of the Cairo Museum, there is a dog. He looks as if he has crept into a small triangle of shade against a wall, as dogs still do nowadays to escape from the hot Egyptian sun, and, leaning against it, has fallen asleep. In fact he died in Egypt about three thousand years ago, but his hair and skin are still well preserved. This kind of natural mummification is possible in the arid desert climate of Egypt when bodies are buried in the sand.

From palaeolithic times man began to develop a dread of death and to believe in an afterlife. This meant that care and ceremony were applied to the burial of the dead, and many of the accoutrements of daily life were interred with the bodies. In the Predynastic period in Egypt (4500-3100 BC), the belief in a continued existence after death, which was to dominate the civilisation for another three thousand years, was probably already established. Cemeteries were situated away from the cultivation and settlements, on low desert spurs along the valley, usually on the west bank of the Nile, which was always associated with the souls of the departed. The graves were shallow oval pits in which the bodies were placed in a crouched or foetal position, the heads normally pointed south with the face turned to the setting sun. Around the body were the grave goods; normally the majority of these were pots of plain and fancy types (black-topped red, red polished, painted), but typically there could also be slate palettes, often in the shape of animals, birds or fish, on which malachite, the green eye cosmetic, was ground. Less frequently there were stone vessels, ivory combs and figurines and objects of copper. Often there were beads and amulets made of various kinds of polished stone, with luxury items such as gold or imported lapis lazuli or turquoise appearing in the richer graves. When the bodies were unprotected from the enclosing sand, a process of swift natural desiccation took place, the decomposition fluids were leached into the sand, and the skin, hair, tendons and ligaments rapidly dried; internally, connective tissue and the larger organs were preserved.

Grave robbing started in Egypt as soon as there were rich graves to be pillaged of their contents. This practice, together with the accidental disturbance of earlier graves in cemeteries as they continued to be used, exposed some bodies and enabled the

Fig. 1. A First Dynasty crouched burial in a mastaba tomb at Tarkhan: the head points to the south and faces west, where there is a niche and a court outside for the offerings.

Egyptians to observe the natural mummification which had taken place. This may have helped to crystallise the belief that in order to survive death it was of paramount importance that the body should continue to exist so that the soul could re-enter it and partake of earthly pleasures.

As the development of civilisation progressed in the late Predynastic, villages, towns and finally cities developed in areas along the valley, precursors to the nome divisions of later times. Local chieftains would have become a powerful elite in charge of agriculture, production and trade, and thereby been in a position to accumulate wealth. This was expressed in the furbishment of the grave and at such important sites as Naqada and Hierakonpolis there were larger, often rectangular, and better equipped graves for the individuals. There was also a general development in the care and comfort afforded to the body. In the Badarian, or early Predynastic, the bodies were merely covered with goat skins, although there were the beginnings of baskets made of twigs around them. Later it became standard practice to place the body on a bier of twigs, or a mat, build a rectangular box structure of twigs and branches around it, and place at least a mat over the top.

The enlargement of the richer graves, often with the use of plank roofing, together with the introduction of air in the space created by this better protection of the bodies, resulted in the opposite effect to that which was desired. By the time that Egypt became unified into a state around 3100 BC, large baskets, in rough wooden coffins or slab pottery box coffins, which held the crouched body wrapped in linen, were contained in large rectangular tombs often lined with plastered mud-brick walls.

It seems that early in the First Dynasty the Egyptians sought to achieve by artificial means some semblance of the preservation of the body which had previously been possible in sand graves. Our material evidence for this is very scanty, mainly because tombs were thoroughly pillaged before excavation, often in early times. At the site of Abydos, which became important in the Early Dynastic period, the royal cemetery had suffered ancient burning and, before its excavation by Flinders Petrie in 1899, it had suffered the fairly typical ransacking investigation of the French Egyptologist Emile Amélineau. He reported finding bodies wrapped in linen impregnated with natron in wooden coffins, but this account and the date of the bodies is very unsure. The first certain piece of evidence for a different technique being used to preserve the body was that of the lower part of an arm (radius and ulna) which Petrie found tucked in a hole in the brick wall of Djer's tomb (First Dynasty). He decided that this was the arm of Djer's queen because it had four bracelets of gold, turquoise and amethyst beads and amulets encircling the wrist, although it could well have been that of the king himself. What is important for the study of the development of mummification is the fact that the arm was wrapped in many layers of fine linen. Unfortunately, although the bracelets are still on display in the Cairo Museum, the then curator, Émile Brugsch, threw away the arm and the linen, exhibiting an attitude to material evidence of the past which Petrie, with his attention to small objects and detailed evidence, had made obsolete; thereby further study was made impossible.

The method of encircling the limbs and digits with layers of fine linen which was impregnated with resin became the standard practice in the Early Dynastic and Old Kingdom. At Saqqara James Quibell found the body of a woman dating from the Second Dynasty with sixteen layers of broad linen bandages, and Walter Emery, also digging the same necropolis later, found a

Fig. 2. The arm wrapped in many layers of linen which Petrie found in the wall of Djer's tomb (First Dynasty) at Abydos. The bracelets are of lapis lazuli, turquoise and gold.

body prepared in this way with the fingers wrapped separately and the breasts and genitals moulded. In this early period the body was still in a semi-flexed position. Within these carefully applied linen bandages there was no tissue left, and often its decomposition had charred the inner surface of the textile, which was then in direct contact with the bones. The aim of the Egyptians at this stage was to create an acceptable resemblance to the living body, and the process employed cannot truly be called embalming. The external features were moulded on the pliable linen, and this method is shown on the foot supposed to be that of King Djoser of the Third Dynasty, which has the tendons modelled in relief over the actual structures. This left foot was found, together with fragments of other bones, by Jean-Philippe Lauer in a granite chamber at the bottom of a deep pit beneath the Step Pyramid of the king at Saqqara in 1934.

In the Third Dynasty (*c*2600 BC) Egypt had entered the pyramid age, commencing with the Step Pyramid and elaborating to the true pyramids of the kings of the Fourth Dynasty. This structure had religious significance in the solar religion of the Old Kingdom, being a symbol of the rays of the sun on which the dead king would mount to the sky to join the sun god Re. It could also represent the primeval mound which first arose from the waters at the beginning of creation. As royal mortuary architecture evolved, so did that of the private tombs; the pyramids became surrounded with the resting places of the nobles, veritable 'mastaba cities'. The rectangular pit tombs of the early periods developed into monuments with superstructures of mud-brick containing store chambers surmounting the burial chamber and other rooms sunk into the rock below. They are called *mastabas* after the low bench seats placed outside modern Arab houses. The store rooms in the mud-brick superstructure were too accessible to plunderers so the upper structure was gradually replaced with solid stone. An essential element in both pyramids and mastabas was the offering place where the mortuary cult for the continued sustenance of the dead could take place. In the pyramid complex the mortuary temple was on the eastern side of the monument, and in the mastabas there was a chapel enclosing an offering niche on the south side of the superstructure.

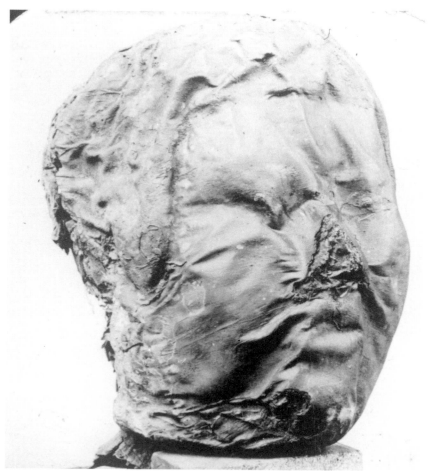

Fig. 3. The head of the Fourth Dynasty noble Ranefer, with painted moulded linen carapace, lost in the bombing of the Royal College of Surgeons during the Second World War.

2
Old Kingdom

In the Fourth Dynasty the next stage in the development towards mummification of the body involved the evisceration of the corpse to inhibit the process of decomposition. In a tomb at Meydum in 1890 Petrie discovered the extended body of a noble called Ranefer who had been covered with linen in the manner already described. His head had been knocked off by plunderers and replaced, supported by a stone. They probably had wished to steal the copper necklace which left a green trace of oxide around the neck. During the early part of the twentieth century this head became famous in the hands of the anatomist Elliot Smith, who had a great interest in the process of mummification. The modelled surface of its linen covering was painted with the hair in black, the eyes and eyebrows in green and the mouth in red. Elliot Smith used to take the head with him to lectures to exhibit the technique and to shake it so that the audience could hear the sound of the dried brain rattling within, a sign that it had not been removed as part of the process. The body was part of the collection of the Royal College of Surgeons in London and unfortunately was lost in bombing during the Second World War. Ranefer was also important for another reason: his body had been eviscerated and the internal organs were wrapped in resin-soaked linen and placed in a recess in the wall of his burial chamber. Many of the tombs at Meydum had such recesses which were empty at the time of excavation.

In 1910 another body was found by Gerald Wainwright in Tomb 17 at Meydum, in a red granite sarcophagus, from which the lid had been prised with an acacia branch. Although the remains were in confusion, it could be seen that the body had been eviscerated, the cavity being packed with vegetable matter. In addition, the brain had been removed from the foraman magnum at the base of the skull. The remains were unusual because the linen bandages went around the vertebrae, the sacrum, the sternum, the scapula and the kneecap, indicating that the bones had been defleshed before wrapping. This, together with other examples, led Petrie to propose that ritual dismemberment had taken place from the Predynastic to the end of the Old Kingdom, with the head being especially revered and retained for family adoration. He quoted from the *Pyramid Texts* (magic spells inscribed on the walls of Fifth and Sixth Dynasty pyramids)

to support the theory:
   Thy dismembered limbs are collected, thou who has might over
   the bows (1018c);
   That I may collect for thee thy flesh, that I might assemble for
   thee thy bones (1884c).
Elliot Smith opposed Petrie's idea and a lively debate took place
between them in the pages of various journals. Elliot Smith
explained the disarticulated bodies as those which had been
found by relatives after the plunderers had been at work and then
subsequently rewrapped. The passages in the Pyramid Texts
which refer to a dismembered body being reassembled allude to
the Osiris legend. Osiris was killed and cut up by his brother Seth
and his various parts were scattered over Egypt until they were
gathered and reconstituted by Isis his consort, and he was
avenged by his son Horus. In the Old Kingdom, the dead king
was assimilated with Osiris, and the living king was Horus; in
later periods, each dead individual became one with Osiris, the
god of the underworld.
   The evidence of the empty recesses in the Meydum tombs,
which signify that the custom of evisceration was widespread, is
paralleled in the necropolis at Giza. In the tomb of Hetepheres,
the mother of Khufu, the builder of the Great Pyramid, there is a
recess which was blocked with masonry set in plaster. The
queen's burial had been moved to Giza from Dashur, and the
famous gilded canopy frame, bed and chair from her tomb are
now in Cairo Museum. Her body was not in the tomb, but in the
recess there was an alabaster chest divided into four compart-
ments resting on a wooden sledge. One compartment was dry and
contained a mass of decayed organic matter; the others had a
yellowish liquid, and analysis showed that it contained a 3 per
cent solution of natron in water (the first evidence of the use of
this salt) and the remains of the organs of the queen. This type of
chest was a precursor to the four containers for the viscera which
became standard in the following dynasties. The organs had to be
placed in the tomb so that the body would be complete, reunited
in the afterlife.
   Prepared bodies dating to the Fifth Dynasty are slightly more
frequent than those known from preceding periods. From the
Fourth Dynasty, the bodies of the royal family and nobles were
interred in an extended position in wooden coffins with fine stone
sarcophagi, frequently decorated on the outside with palace
facade panelling. George Reisner, an American Egyptologist,
excavated numerous tombs in the necropolis of Giza. In Shaft B

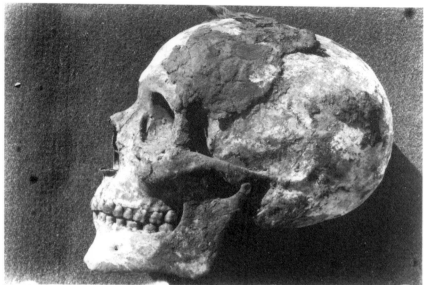

Fig. 4. The skull from Tomb 17 at Meydum (which was broken up while travelling): it had remains of linen and hair; Fourth Dynasty.
Fig. 5. Meydum, Tomb 17: (Left) the mass of wrapping from the base of the skull with bandages around and between the bones; (Top right) the penis modelled in cloth; (Bottom right) a globular pad of cloth from an eye socket.

Fig. 6. The mummy in the tomb of Nefer at Saqqara with modelled stucco plastered linen and beads *in situ;* Fifth Dynasty. (Courtesy of German Institute, Cairo.)

of Tomb 2220 in 1933 he found the extended body of a woman in a well preserved wooden coffin. She had been wrapped for burial in the usual Old Kingdom style with the features of her face modelled in linen bandages and painted, and there were one or two other embellishments. She wore a long V-necked sleeveless dress which reached almost to her ankles, where her feet, with their separately bandaged toes, peeped out; her arms were extended to her sides. On removal of the dress by the anatomist Douglas Derry, it was revealed that her entire bosom had been modelled in a criss-crossed linen with the nipples reproduced like buttons on the linen breast. In this case it seems that the abdominal organs had not been removed, and there was very little tissue left beneath the bandages. Hollows had been padded out with wads of linen and one piece was inscribed with the phrase 'fine linen'. The body of Nenkheftka of the Fifth Dynasty, found by Petrie at Deshasheh, was of the same genre, having the male sexual organs modelled in cloth and placed in position.

Another mummy of the Fifth Dynasty has received some publicity. Two mummies were found in a rock tomb at Saqqara in 1966 inscribed with the names Nefer and Kahay. The male, who is now known as the 'earliest mummified body', has taken the name of Nefer, although the tomb was a multiple burial place with eleven shafts, and he was accompanied by a wooden box with the name of Watay, chief of weavers, probably a contemporary of Nefer's sons. The body still lies in a wooden coffin in the base of Shaft 8 on the east side of the tomb where it was discovered. As usual it had been wrapped in linen which was then moulded, but in this case stucco plaster was used; the genitalia were particularly well modelled. The wig, eyes, eyebrows and moustache are painted and there is a linen false beard. There is a mass of green faience beads around the neck, and the whole torso has a green tinge. Watay was one of the mummies X-rayed between 1966 and 1971 by a team from the University of Michigan, whose results are discussed further in the section on New Kingdom mummies. His X-ray revealed that his teeth are in excellent condition, which was unusual for ancient Egyptians, and he was middle-aged at death.

Petrie had pioneered the use of X-rays in 1898 as a non-destructive technique to study mummified remains. At Deshasheh he discovered Fifth Dynasty burials which showed signs of dismemberment, or at least subsequent rewrapping in which

Fig. 7. (Below) The pioneering X-ray of the reassembled Deshasheh bones taken by Petrie in 1898 (UC 31179-31180); Fifth Dynasty. *(Left)* Misplaced foot bones. *(Right)* Two tibia, one ulna.
Fig. 8. (Right) The Deshasheh bones in the X-ray which were dismembered and rewrapped (UC 31179-31180).

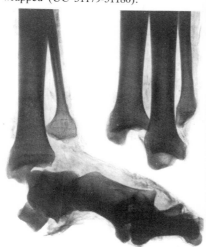

Fig. 9. An Old Kingdom reserve head of plaster, provided as a substitute should the mummy be damaged (UC 15988).

the bones had been misplaced. He used an X-ray to record the proof that the wrapped foot has the bones out of order, and that the leg and arm bones are wrapped together. These bones, which still have the bandages around them, are preserved in his collection at University College, London (UC 31179-80, from Deshasheh tombs 113 and 115 respectively).

The method of preserving the body by external wrapping and modelling in linen remained standard through the Sixth Dynasty. A woman's body of that date in a dress, with painted braces in white and painted anklets, bracelets and necklace in green, was found in the mastaba of Kaenesu at Saqqara, but it fell to pieces on removal from the grave. Another male mummy was that of Setka found at Giza, and this was examined by the anatomist Derry, who found that the skin had decomposed leaving only the shredded remains and had 'burned' the inner surface of the linen. Plaster was occasionally used on the external surface of the linen to model the features, particularly the heads, instead of resin. The embalmers of this age were not able to preserve the body, but in this way they transformed it into a virtual statue which could also be entered by the spirit. In addition to the attention paid to transforming the body, reserve heads of plaster were provided as a kind of back-up, and portrait busts or statues were also depicted in the central recesses of the false doors. These solid doors were stelae forming the focal point of the offering chapel through which the deceased's *ka,* one of his two main souls, could receive the offerings; they were frequently decorated with a scene of the owner of the tomb before a table piled high with

Fig. 10. Scenes of mourning and the funeral from a Sixth Dynasty tomb: (Top left) the female mourners; (Top right) the male mourners; (Bottom) the coffin being dragged to the tomb (after Simpson, W. K. *The Mastabas of Qar and Idu,* 1976, fig. 35).

provisions. Lifelike portrait statues, which served as substitute bodies should an accident befall the mummy, were also walled up in chambers called *serdabs,* through which holes were cut at eye level so that the statue could look out. An early example of one such statue is that of King Djoser found in the serdab of the mortuary temple of his pyramid. This statue, now in Cairo (there is a duplicate within the serdab at Saqqara), had it eyes gouged out; they would have been inlaid with translucent stones, thereby creating an all-seeing animation in the statue.

It is known from Old Kingdom tomb reliefs, and from those of the New Kingdom, that tremendous ceremony accompanied the process of mummification and burial and that the magic employed was at least as important as the techniques of embalming. Each stage of the proceedings was accompanied by an appropriate ritual, the most important of which was the final ceremony at the tomb in front of the portrait statue, and later the mummy, of the deceased. This was the Ritual of Opening the Mouth, the purpose of which was to restore the powers of sight, hearing and speech to the body; in other words, to bring it back to life. This was based on the legend of Osiris when his son Horus was the first to perform the ceremony for the reassembled body of his father. Traditionally a son performed it for his father, thereby also confirming his inheritance.

From this survey of the processes employed, and from the reasons which led to the art of mummification, it can be seen that the accoutrements of the resting place were vital as an evironment for the deceased. Old Kingdom tombs not only have the texts of the various rituals and ceremonies involved inscribed on their walls, but also repetitive scenes of the offerings being brought to the owner, as a magic safeguard should the mortuary cult not continue in perpetuity. The incumbent was also magically provided with the means to produce sustenance. Scenes of agriculture, herding, hunting, butchery, fishing, baking and brewing ensured that provisions would be continually available. Fashions in tomb design changed through Egypt's long history, but these basic magical elements remained the same, embellished occasionally with records of important events which had taken place during the owner's life. Should all other provisions fail, the one essential was that the name of the person be preserved, either in writing or in verbal repetition, so he could continue to live in his tomb. The Egyptians loved life and believed that the acquisition and equipping of a tomb was an essential practical step in order to extend it for eternity.

3
Middle Kingdom

There is little evidence for mummification from the politically disunified First Intermediate Period, but bodies wrapped in linen, some with cartonnage masks, and canopic jars were found at Saqqara, dating to the Ninth to Eleventh Dynasties. In the Eleventh Dynasty control by central government was re-exerted by a family in the Theban area, and the Middle Kingdom began. The Metropolitan Museum undertook investigations of the Theban west bank temples and necropolises during the 1920s. A group of mummies of Eleventh Dynasty princesses was found in rock-cut tombs at Deir el-Bahri, signifying that an improvement in technique had taken place. Their bodies were rapidly desiccated with dry natron, which is a naturally occurring salt in Egypt composed of sodium carbonate (or bicarbonate) and sodium chloride (or sulphate). This ensured the preservation of the tissues and then the surface of the skin was coated with resin. They were not eviscerated however, and it seems from the dilated rectum and vagina that an oleo-resin (akin to turpentine) was injected into the anus in order to dissolve the organs for removal. Most scholars identify this procedure as the second, cheaper method of embalming described by the Greek historian Herodotus, but it may simply be that evisceration of the abdominal organs through an incision was a northern Egyptian technique and was not brought into use in Middle Egypt again until the country was reunified. The princesses are also interesting because some of them are tattooed, the only instance of the practice found on ancient Egyptian bodies, although it is depicted on Predynastic figurines. This may be an Upper Egyptian, or even Nubian, custom; it seems that there was Nubian blood in the royal family.

Sixty soldiers who fell in a battle to subdue the north under Nebheptre Mentuhotep II of the Eleventh Dynasty were brought back to Thebes for burial. The wounded, decomposed bodies were torn at by birds and there is sand adhering to them, which seem to have been the rough and ready method employed to dry them. No further attention was paid to them other than linen wrappings, and it may well be that this simple treatment of the body was general practice with poorer individuals.

The estate manager Wah was buried at Thebes during the reign of the last king of the Eleventh Dynasty, Sankhare Mentuhotep III. His tomb was undisturbed, and his mummy lay in a wooden

coffin covered with a linen shawl as a kilt. It was unwrapped in
1935 at the Metropolitan Museum. Under the shawl were spiral
bandages around the body, which looked cigar-shaped at this
stage. Beneath these bandages were sheets and pads and a gilded
stucco mask, then a layer of dark resin. Fine necklaces of
semi-precious stones, gold and silver at this level are now on
display in the Metropolitan Museum. Four scarabs were found
over the crossed arms on the chest, one of faience, two of silver
and one of lapis lazuli. One of the silver scarabs was inscribed for
Wah and Prince Meket-Re, whose tomb with its famous models
had already been discovered. Beneath the resin were further
bandages over more resin, and then a broad collar of faience
beads and bracelets on the individually wrapped arms. A total of
375 square metres (4036 square feet) of linen, many pieces
bearing Wah's name, was removed from the body; some of it
bore the emblamer's fingerprints in the resin. Whilst working on
the body the embalmers had allowed a mouse, a lizard and a
cricket to become entangled in the wrappings. The body was
eviscerated through an incision in the abdomen, but the organs
were left intact above the diaphragm, and the brain was still in
place. Wah died at about thirty years of age.

  Near the entrance to the tomb of a man called Ipy was a sealed
chamber which contained a cache of embalmers' materials left
over from his mummification. These caches are also known from
later periods, and it seems that this refuse had to be gathered and
preserved near, but not in, the tomb, so that any scraps of the
body would be retained for its completion. In this case there were
sixty-seven pottery jars containing bags of natron salt, oils and
sawdust, which had been carried up to the cavity on slings, and
the last load had been dumped with the wooden yoke. On top of
the pottery and cloths was a broken embalming table, the
dismantled boards of which were reconstructed to make a table 7
feet 11 inches (2.41 m) long and 4 feet 2½ inches (1.28 m) wide.
On top of it were four rectangular wooden blocks to support the
body, spaced out at intervals across its width. Separately carved
ankh (life) signs were placed in each corner and the whole surface
was stained with natron and oils.

  In the Twelfth Dynasty (from about 2000 BC) the process of
mummification became further elaborated and the technique
approached that of the New Kingdom, although significant
advances in preservation had to wait until the latter period. All
the organs, except for the heart, were removed from two bodies
found at Saqqara, and the cavity was stuffed with linen, which

Fig. 11. The Twelfth Dynasty coffin of the eunuch Nekht Ankh from Rifeh, now in the Manchester Museum.

Fig. 12. Models from the tomb of Khnum Nakht and Nekht Ankh from Rifeh: (i) Khnum Nakht; (ii) Nekht Ankh; (iii and iv) female offering bearers; (v) Nekht Ankh.

was also pushed beneath the eyelids. The tissues were not well preserved, but the face of the man was coated with resin, including plugs in the nostrils, and he had a beard and moustache. The Lady Senebtisi, found at Lisht, also had her viscera removed from a flank incision, which was then sealed with a resin-soaked cloth. Her heart had been packed with linen and replaced in her body, together with linen and sawdust soaked in resin. The four canopic jars, which by this time had human heads, were found in a rotted canopic chest, and only two of them had contents, all of which were in resinous masses, resembling human organs: one perhaps the liver, another a parcel of intestines.

The bodies of two half-brothers from an intact Twelfth Dynasty tomb at Rifeh, discovered by Ernest Mackay in 1907, were sent to Manchester Museum, where their detailed investigation by Margaret Murray produced interesting results, although the tissues were virtually gone. One of the bodies had the nails tied on with thread to prevent their loss during the desiccation process; this became standard practice in the Middle Kingdom. This man was called Nekht Ankh; he was about sixty years of age at death and his skeleton and possible remains of his genital organs suggested that he was a eunuch. His brother, Khnum

Nakht, had negro blood and suffered from osteo-arthritis and palsy; he was about forty at death. Further scientific work was undertaken on the skeletons of these two men during the Manchester Mummy Project work in the 1970s, during which reconstructions of their heads were compared to their statuettes. They had shared a canopic chest, but only two of the jars contained traces of the organs.

Rock tombs were not uncommon in the Old Kingdom, but they gained in popularity during the First Intermediate Period. In this type of funerary structure both the sepulchre and the chapel were cut into the rock of desert cliffs. By the Middle Kingdom, decorated rock-cut chapel tombs belonging to district governors were driven into the cliffs at various places in Middle and Upper Egypt. They consisted of a decorated facade, sometimes with a columned portico, leading to a pillared hall and a shrine at the end for the portrait statue of the deceased; the burial chamber was in a pit at a lower level. The walls of these tombs were

Fig. 13. The canopic chest shared by Khnum Nakht and Nekht Ankh; only two of the jars contained traces of the organs.

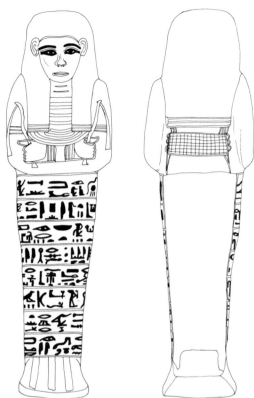

Fig. 14. A painted wooden shabti of the Eighteenth Dynasty with hoes and a basket for corvée work in the afterworld.

decorated with painted reliefs to guarantee the supply of offerings, and these were reinforced by the use of models, which were very much in vogue during the Middle Kingdom. The majority of model groups of figures illustrate scenes of baking, brewing and agriculture, and model boats with oars and sails are also common. One of the model scenes from the tomb of Meket-Re of the Eleventh Dynasty has phalanxes of fine painted wooden Nubian soldiers, complete with bows and arrows and cowhide shields.

New kinds of funerary figurine also appeared, called *shabtis,* whose task it was to undertake work that might be assigned to the deceased in the underworld. In the Middle Kingdom these inscribed mummiform figures were roughly made of wood and enclosed in a wooden model coffin. In the New Kingdom they became more elaborate and were made of painted wood, stone or blue faience; they can be dated stylistically to various dynasties.

By that time, the original single shabti of the Middle Kingdom had become a large group organised into gangs under overseer shabtis, who were distinguished by their whips; ordinary shabtis had hoes and baskets for work in the Elysian fields.

The Pyramid Texts of the Old Kingdom pharaohs were adapted for widespread use in the Middle Kingdom. They were painted on wooden coffins *(Coffin Texts)* and provide spells to protect the deceased and ensure his survival, as well as a guide for his journey beyond. The external decoration of the coffin included a horizontal text below the rim with a prayer for offerings, and the name of the owner and panels of vertical texts at the sides giving standard funerary inscriptions. At the left side, level with the head, there was a painting of two sacred eyes, either alone or above an elaborate palace facade doorway. These represented the eyes of Horus, and within the coffin the body was turned on to its left side so that the painted eyes could enable him to see out. The noble Wah was found in his coffin in this position and the unwrapped body of the Lady Inenit of the Eleventh Dynasty in the Cairo Museum still has her head twisted to this side. The sky goddess Nut was identified with the lid of the coffin and she was painted spread over the body to protect it. Within the coffin was a painted scene of the sun god in his boat traversing the sky on the underside of the lid, and the floor had scenes from the underworld.

Cartonnage face masks, made of waste papyrus or linen soaked in plaster, similar to *papier maché,* with a painted or gilded surface, and placed over the head of the mummy, became fashionable in the Middle Kingdom. These may represent a link with the surface mouldings on the linen employed during the Old Kingdom. Another innovation was the introduction of the

Fig. 15. A Middle Kingdom wooden coffin with a prayer for offerings, funerary texts and the eye panel so that the incumbent could see out.

anthropoid coffin, usually fitted within the rectangular box coffin; it copied the mummy in form and further identified the deceased with Osiris. In the Second Intermediate Period, the outer coffin was discontinued and the anthropoid coffin elaborated into the *rishi* type with the outspread wings of the goddesses Isis and Nepthys as kites protecting and mourning the dead person. In the New Kingdom the anthropoid coffin became standard with painted religious scenes between bands across the body and an integral face mask framed by a heavy wig; time produced even more elaborate decoration and the cartonnage masks, which began in the Middle Kingdom, extended into equally well covered body cases.

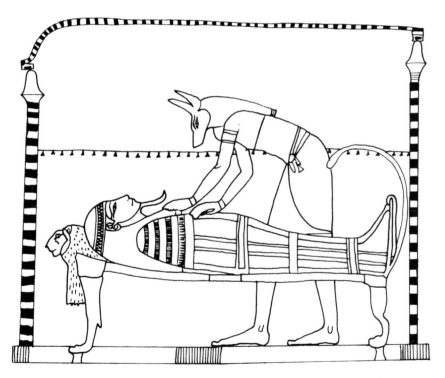

Fig. 16. Anubis, the patron god of embalmers, preparing the mummy in the tomb of Sennedjem at Deir el-Medina, Nineteenth Dynasty.

4
Mummification and the funeral in the New Kingdom

From the day of death to the funeral seventy days elapsed, during which time mummification and the accompanying ceremonies took place. This period of seventy days seems to have been standard until the Roman period and is connected with the heliacal rising of the dog star Sirius, the herald of the vital Nile flood.

At first the body was taken to the *Per-Nefer,* the House of Mummification, where the first stages of the process took place. The corpse was laid on the embalming table and the decomposed softened brain was teased through the nostril with a metal hook after the ethmoid bone had been broken. Then an incision was made in the left side of the abdomen by the cutter and the lower organs, except for the kidneys, were removed by the embalmer. The patron god of the skilled embalmers, the jackal-headed Anubis, was often shown in tomb scenes ministering to the mummy. The diaphragm was cut and all but the heart, the 'seat of the mind', was removed from the chest cavity. The internal organs were washed and soaked separately in natron, then treated with hot resin, bandaged, and packed in the four canopic jars. The lids of these jars represented the four sons of Horus: Imsety, who was human-headed, guarded the liver; Hapy, ape-headed, guarded the lungs; Dwamutef, jackal-headed, guarded the stomach; and Qebhsenuef, falcon-headed, the intestines. The cavity left was cleaned, most probably with palm wine and spices, then stuffed with temporary packing material and the body was desiccated with heaps of dry natron. The toe and finger nails were secured with string to prevent loss during the drying. The process up to this point probably took about forty days, and then the body was delivered to the *Wabet,* the House of Purification, where it was washed with Nile water, a ritualised procedure to symbolise the rising of the sun from the river and the subsidence of the inundation waters. Then the cranial cavity was stuffed with resin-soaked linen, and the body cavity, emptied of temporary packing, was packed with linen bags of sawdust or myrrh soaked in resin, and the abdominal incision was sewn up. The surface of the body was rubbed with a mixture of cedar oil, wax, natron and gum, and then dusted with spices. The nose was

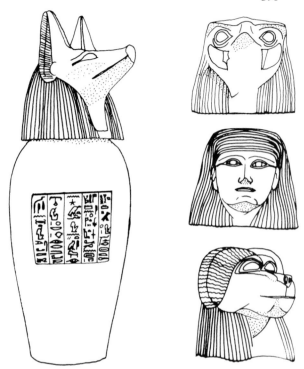

Fig. 17. A set of canopic jars with the heads of Dwamutef (jackal), Qebhsenuef (falcon), Imsety (human) and Hapy (baboon).

plugged, and frequently pads of linen were inserted under the eyelids, although onions were sometimes used. The whole body was then coated with molten resin to close the pores and protect the surface; this resulted in the superior preservation attained in the New Kingdom, so noticeable when compared to the tissue loss on the bodies of earlier periods.

The bandaging of the body was a deliberate process over the latter part of the allotted seventy days; the extant Late Period and Roman texts detail the necessary incantations which accompanied the process. It seems that the embalming was over by the fifty-second day, and the coffining took place on the sixty-eighth to seventieth day. Spells were recited as each limb was separately bandaged and then the torso; frequently an enveloping shroud was wrapped around the body and then the bandaging continued.

As the layered bandaging grew, amulets were placed in position, and these are now detected *in situ* on mummies by X-ray techniques without the need to unwrap them, as was sometimes done in the past. The Coffin Texts of the Middle Kingdom formed the basis of the New Kingdom *Book of the Dead* (Chapters of Coming Forth by Day), written on a roll of papyrus and placed in the coffin with the deceased. Spells within this funerary book, often illustrated with vignettes during the Nineteenth Dynasty, contained instructions for correct and safe procedures through the underworld and included notes on the recommended amulets to protect the dead person. Spells concerning the heart, which was considered the seat of the mind and emotion, were particularly important, and Spells 30 *a* and *b* were frequently inscribed on the large green heart scarabs placed on the body. The heart was instructed not to render evidence against the deceased during the final judgement, during which it would be placed in the balance and weighed against the feather of Maat, goddess of truth and right. The *djed* pillar amulet, representing the backbone of Osiris, was to be placed on the neck and also the *tyet* amulet, the girdle tie of Isis, and the green papyrus column. The head-rest amulet, frequently made of

Fig. 18. The ritual lustration of Djehuty-hotep from his tomb at El-Bersheh, Twelfth Dynasty (after Newberry, P. E. *El Bersheh*, 1894, plate X).

haematite, was placed under the head, and the *udjat* eye of Horus appeared as an individual amulet or on the plate placed over the embalming incision. All these amulets and others, such as the *ankh* sign, served a magical purpose in protecting the individual and renewing his specific strengths.

The mummy was then placed in its coffin on a sledge beneath a shrine and transported on a ferry to the west bank of the Nile where it was then drawn by oxen and men. Two women representing the goddesses Isis and Nepthys, called the Great and Little Kites, proceeded with the sledge, accompanied by a band of mourners and priests, with libations of milk being poured before the way. All the grave goods were carried by servants at the rear behind a second sledge transporting the canopic chest.

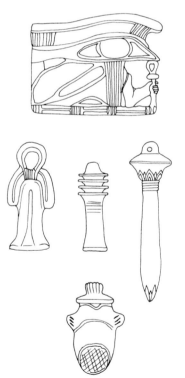

Fig. 19. A group of amulets: *udjat* eye with *ankh* sign, *tyet* knot of Isis, *djed* pillar of Osiris, papyrus column and heart.

Fig. 20. A heart scarab with a Chapter of the Book of the Dead inscribed on its base.

Fig. 21. The Ritual of Opening the Mouth from the tomb of Nakhtamun at Thebes, Nineteenth Dynasty (after de Garis Davies, *Seven Private Tombs at Kurnah*, 1948, plate XXVI).

At the tomb the procession was met by a group of dancers and a lector priest. The anthropoid case containing the mummy was placed upright facing the mourners, held by a priest wearing the jackal head of Anubis. Then the vitally important Ritual of Opening the Mouth took place, which completed the body, restored its functions and resurrected it for eternal existence. The The *Sem*-priest, as 'the son whom-he-loves', touched the mouth of the mummy with ritual instruments including an adze and a forked knife. Censing and libation took place and also the sacrifice of an ox; clothing, ointment and food were offered to the deceased.

Finally the mourners enjoyed a lavish feast (compare Irish wakes), entertained by musicians and dancers performing songs of praise for the dead. While this was taking place, the mummy was installed in the burial chamber, and a priest impersonating the god Thoth swept the floor in order to expunge all the footprints. (Twigs from this broom were found in the Middle Kingdom tomb of Wah.) Everything that had touched the mummy, including the embalming materials, was gathered up and buried a short distance from the tomb. Now the deceased's *ba,* as a human-headed bird, could fly away from the body by day to return at night, and the *ka,* his double or life force, who lived in the tomb, could go to the chapel and receive food offerings, should the descendants have been diligent enough to ensure them for eternity.

Fig. 22. Head of Queen Tetisheri showing maxillary prognathism (buck teeth), Seventeenth Dynasty (from Elliot Smith, *Cairo Catalogue: Royal Mummies,* 1912).

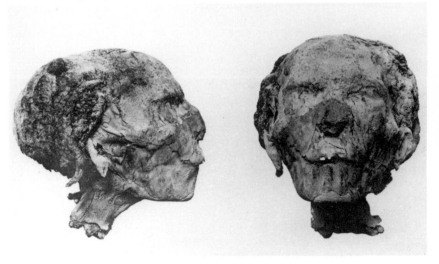

5
Second Intermediate and New Kingdom mummies

For the Second Intermediate and New Kingdom periods, the collection of royal mummies in the Cairo Museum, Egypt, provides a wealth of information. Their discovery is described in Chapter 6. Between 1966 and 1971 the mummies were the subject of investigations by X-ray which added more to our knowledge of the physical condition of the royal families of the Eighteenth, Nineteenth and Twentieth Dynasties. Only a brief description of the main rulers can be given here; for more detail the reader is referred to the volumes in the bibliography.

The founders of the powerful line of New Kingdom rulers were commoners who ruled in Thebes at the end of the Seventeenth Dynasty. They were responsible for the expulsion of the Hyksos, foreign invaders resident in the Delta, and for the founding of the New Kingdom. Tetisheri, the queen from whom the later pharaohs were descended through consanguineous (brother-sister) marriage, exhibits the buck teeth shown by her female descendants through four generations. Her scanty white hair was interwoven with artificial braids to cover a bald patch, an artifice later used on other female mummies. Her son, Seqenenre Tao, engaged in battle against the despised Hyksos; the state of his body would seem to confirm this because it is the most grotesque of the royal mummies. His face is fixed in death spasms and the head has extensive wounds made by clubs, maces and axes. Recent X-rays have revealed that the bone around one axe blow on the forehead had partly regrown. This blow, which Seqenenre seems to have survived, probably caused the evident paralysis in one arm. His body was hastily and insufficiently embalmed and is the least well preserved of the royal mummies.

He had married Tetisheri's daughter Aahotep and produced a number of children before his untimely death; one of them, Kamose, became king and continued to fight against the Hyksos. This campaign was successfully continued by Ahmose I and led to their withdrawal and his identification as the first king of the Eighteenth Dynasty, although there had been no change in the ruling family. His mummy exhibits a method of brain removal similar to that which sometimes took place in the Old Kingdom. The brain was removed via the foramen magnum, the hole at the

Fig. 23. (Left) Head of Seqenenre Tao II showing the severe head wounds inflicted in battle, Seventeenth Dynasty (from Elliot Smith, *Cairo Catalogue: Royal Mummies*, 1912).
Fig. 24. (Right) The mummy of Ahmose I, Eighteenth Dynasty, who was uncircumcised (from Elliot Smith, *Cairo Catalogue: Royal Mummies*, 1912).
Fig. 25. (Below) Queen Ahmose-Nefertari, wife of Ahmose I, Eighteenth Dynasty (from Elliot Smith, *Cairo Catalogue: Royal Mummies*, 1912).

base of the skull, and the atlas vertebra is missing. Ahmose's body was covered with thick resin, but recent X-rays have revealed that he suffered from arthritis in his knees and back, and also that he was uncircumcised, an unusual state among Egyptian males. He married a half-sister, Ahmose-Nefertari, who lived to an old age, and who also had her scanty hair interwoven with false braids and a marked maxillary protrusion like Tetisheri. Her X-ray revealed the presence of scoliosis (curvature of the spine).

The son of Ahmose and Ahmose-Nefertari was Amenophis I, whose mummy has never been unwrapped and still wears a fine cartonnage mask. It is known that he was the first pharaoh to separate his mortuary temple from his tomb, although neither structure has been found. His prominent dentition confirms the family resemblance, and his sister-wife, Ahmose Meryet-Amun, who died in her twenties, had arthritis and scoliosis. The arms of Ahmose and his queen had been extended by their sides, but from the time of Amenophis I the custom was to cross them on the breast. This fashion, together with the age of a mummy initially identified as Tuthmosis I, has led scholars to doubt its identification; its arms are extended to the genital region. From textual evidence, the king lived for about fifty years and the mummy is that of a young man. He does, however, show great similarity to Tuthmosis II, his son, who died at an early age and whose body shows he was a frail individual, covered with unidentified scabrous patches.

Tuthmosis III has been dubbed the Napoleon of the New Kingdom for he excelled as a general conquering foreign lands and as an administrator; he was also an accomplished athlete. His mummy shows him to have been of medium build, about 5 feet (1.5 m) tall with worn but intact teeth and a large cranial cavity. His son Amenophis II boasted of his prowess in hunting, and the bow which he claimed that no one else could string or pull was found in his coffin. He was taller than his father and his son and was about forty-five when he died. There is evidence that he suffered from ankylosing spondylitis, and there are nodules on his torso which suggest a disease. He was succeeded by his son, Tuthmosis IV, who was responsible for clearing the sand away from the Great Sphinx at Giza and was thereby assured the throne by the god incarnate, Re-Harakhte. His mummy still possesses an ethereal quality suggestive of a thoughtful man, but its state of emaciation is extreme. His arms are crossed on his chest and his hands show that they once grasped the emblems of royalty, the crook and flail. Both he and his father have skin

Fig. 26. (Left) The mummy of Amenophis I, which is still unwrapped, Eighteenth Dynasty (from Elliot Smith, *Cairo Catalogue: Royal Mummies,* 1912).

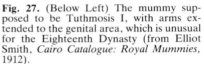

Fig. 27. (Below Left) The mummy supposed to be Tuthmosis I, with arms extended to the genital area, which is unusual for the Eighteenth Dynasty (from Elliot Smith, *Cairo Catalogue: Royal Mummies,* 1912).
Fig. 28. (Below) Tuthmosis II, Eighteenth Dynasty (from Elliot Smith, *Cairo Catalogue: Royal Mummies,* 1912).

Fig. 29. The conquering pharaoh Tuthmosis III, Eighteenth Dynasty (from Elliot Smith, *Cairo Catalogue: Royal Mummies,* 1912).

darkened by the application of resin, a common effect during this period. The mummy labelled as Tuthmosis IV's son, Amenophis III, was badly hacked by tomb robbers, and some scholars believe he may be Akhenaten (Amenophis IV). Enough remains of this individual to indicate that he was a fat sedentary man before his death with alveolar abscesses and heavy tartar deposits on his teeth, indicating a rich and sweet diet at the royal court. His wife, Queen Tiye, has been tentatively identified as the 'Elder Lady' found in the tomb of Amenophis II, because of a similarity to Thuya, her mother. The commoners who were her parents gained a tomb in the Valley of the Kings at Thebes. Their mummies, which did not suffer the excesses of the resin application applied to the royal bodies, are the most excellently preserved of the Eighteenth Dynasty. Yuya's body is so well-preserved that a short growth of reddish-blond beard is evident on his chin. Thuya, his wife, also had reddish-blond hair, and both suffered with bad teeth like their son-in-law.

The tomb of Tutankhamun is the best known in the Valley of the Kings and the smallest. The discovery of the tomb and its wondrous grave goods by Howard Carter and Lord Carnarvon in 1922 has been the subject of numerous publications. The young king's body was not only intact within his solid gold coffin and funerary mask but also rested within two outer mummiform coffins, a sarcophagus and four golden shrines. Such lavish protection, which included 143 amulets within the bandaging, did

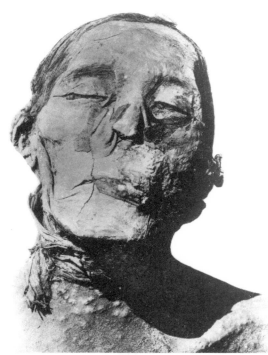

Fig. 30. (Left) Amenophis II, in whose tomb a cache of royal mummies was discovered (from *Annales du Service*, III, plate 1).

Fig. 31. (Below) Tuthmosis IV, who was extremely emaciated, Eighteenth Dynasty (from Elliot Smith, *Cairo Catalogue: Royal Mummies*, 1912).

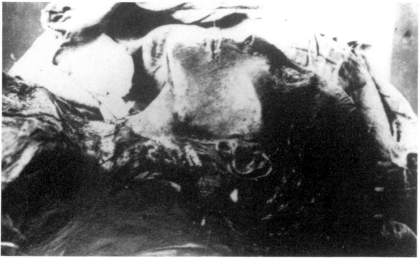

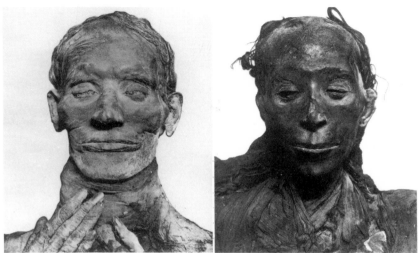

Fig. 32. (Left) Yuya, the father of Queen Tiye, with whiskers, Eighteenth Dynasty (from Quibell, J. E.*The Tomb of Yuaa and Thuiu,* 1908).
Fig. 33. (Right) Thuya, the mother of Queen Tiye, Eighteenth Dynasty (from Quibell, J. E.*The Tomb of Yuaa and Thuiu,* 1908.

not ensure the good preservation of the body, which had been burned by the lavish application of resinous liquid. The king was about eighteen to twenty years old when he died; his upper and lower wisdom teeth had just erupted, but his body does not show any pathological conditions which would have caused his death. His cache of embalming materials was found in 1908 (before his tomb was discovered) and included the remains of the funerary repast: nine chickens, four geese, a shoulder of beef, sheep ribs and the floral collars worn by the mourners. His body still lies in his tomb.

The most impressive royal mummy is that of Seti I of the Nineteenth Dynasty, the second king of a new royal family. His well preserved head still shows the nobility of the king, whose tomb is the longest of those cut into the walls of the Valley of the Kings. His son, Ramesses II, is well known for the self-aggrandisement he indulged in over a reign of sixty-seven years; he is the 'Ozymandias' of Shelley's poem and was the builder of the rock-hewn temples of Abu Simbel. His mummy confirms a great age at death (over ninety) and the suffering that went with it: degenerative arthritis of the hip and arteriosclerosis of the arteries in the feet, as well as painful alveolar abscesses in the jaw. His mummy travelled to Paris in 1977 for an exhibition,

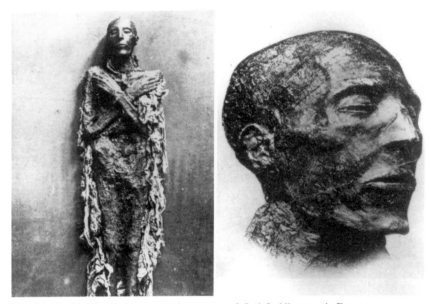

Fig. 34. (Left) The well preserved mummy of Seti I, Nineteenth Dynasty.
Fig. 35. (Right) The fine head of Seti I, Nineteenth Dynasty.

where it underwent conservation. Merneptah was Ramesses II's thirteenth son and was middle-aged when he succeeded to the throne. The X-ray of his mummy clearly shows the extensive vascular calcification of arteriosclerosis. He shared with his father bad dental health and the hooked nose, which was a family characteristic. His mummy has one or two unusual features. There was a hole in the side of the head, probably made after death, and the scrotum is mysteriously missing, the wound being covered with resin, perhaps after the excision of a hernia. Salt encrustation on his skin caused by natron led early scholars to believe that, as the pharaoh of the Exodus, he had drowned in the Red Sea. Both Seti II and Siptah, who followed Merneptah, had good dentition, but Siptah had a deformed left foot, which has recently been identified as caused by poliomyelitis; he died in his early twenties.

Apart from his historical fame as the pharaoh who repulsed the Sea People's invasion of Egypt, Ramesses III of the Twentieth Dynasty has gained another kind of immortality, for his mummy was used as the model for many modern horror films. His arms

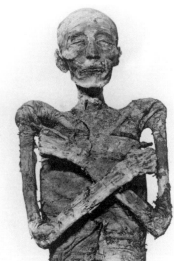

Fig. 36. (Above) Ramesses II, who was over ninety at his death, Nineteenth Dynasty.
Fig. 37. (Above Right) Merneptah, the pharaoh of the Exodus, Nineteenth Dynasty (from Elliot Smith, *Cairo Catalogue: Royal Mummies*, 1912).

Fig. 38. (Right) Siptah, showing his deformed foot caused by poliomyelitis, Nineteenth Dynasty (from Elliot Smith, *Cairo Catalogue: Royal Mummies*, 1912).

Fig. 39. (Left) Ramesses III, the model for modern horror films, Twentieth Dynasty (from Elliot Smith, *Cairo Catalogue: Royal Mummies,* 1912).
Fig. 40. (Right) Ramesses V, showing the smallpox pustules on his face, Twentieth Dynasty (from Elliot Smith, *Cairo Catalogue: Royal Mummies,* 1912).

are crossed on his chest with the palms opened, superseding the previous fashion for closed fists holding the flail and sceptre. X-rays have revealed that there are still three funerary figurines of the four sons of Horus in his thorax; wrapping the viscera around the genii and re-inserting them in the body was to become common practice in the Twenty-First Dynasty. His Ramesside successors, who brought the New Kingdom to a close, were numerous and short-reigned. Of them, Ramesses V's mummy is noteworthy because the skin still bears the papular eruptions typical of smallpox; he died in his early thirties. Ramesses IV's abdominal cavity had been packed with dried lichens, as had Siptah's, but Ramesses V's body was stuffed with sawdust containing portions of the internal organs, together with spices which still perfume the body. The body of Ramesses VI suffered greatly in the hands of tomb robbers and was repaired and rewrapped during the Twenty-First Dynasty with two miscellaneous right hands included in the bandages.

6
Twenty-First Dynasty and later periods

During the reign of Ramesses XI the appalling sacrilege in the royal necropolis reached an unacceptable level and efforts were made to bring tomb robbers to trial. The ancient craft of tomb robbing was probably condoned by the necropolis guards and priests, but Pa-ser, the mayor of east Thebes, obtained confessions and forced an inquiry. Eventually forty-five men were brought to trial and the transcript was recorded on papyri, which themselves were stolen from Theban tombs and ended up on the Luxor antiquities market. The violations horrified the priest-kings of the Twenty-First Dynasty, founded by Herihor, who took precautions to safeguard the royal mummies and moved them to secret hiding places.

The modern Arab village of Sheikh Abd el-Qurneh is on the slopes of the ancient Theban necropolis above the Tombs of the Nobles and not far from the Valley of the Kings and the Valley of the Queens to the west. Continuing the traditions of three thousand years ago, the villagers of Qurneh made a living from plundering the tombs and selling objects to the antiquities dealers in Luxor across the river. This traffic became especially profitable after the 1860s when European travellers created a demand. Ahmed and Mohammed Abd el-Rassoul discovered a cache of mummies and burial objects in a shaft at Deir el-Bahri in 1871 and lived for a decade on the proceeds, earned by selling the objects a few at a time. Eventually the unusual items came to the attention of Gaston Maspero, Director of the Egyptian Antiquities Service, and in 1881 Mohammed revealed where the cache was located. It contained the mummies of New Kingdom royalty, some with labels, telling of their reburial by the priests of the Twenty-First Dynasty, together with a token number of the objects which had originally belonged to them. The bodies were brought out of the crypt immediately and taken to Cairo by boat, accompanied by the wailing of a traditional funeral from fellahin on the river banks. This tale is evocatively told by the Egyptian film maker Shadi Abdelsalam in his film *The Night of the Counting of the Years*.

In 1898 Victor Loret found another cache of royal mummies in the tomb of Amenophis II. All these mummies were taken to Cairo, save that of the owner of the tomb, but his torso was broken into and the body robbed by the same team of established

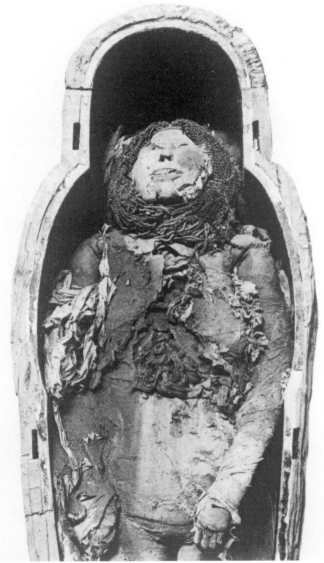

Fig. 41. Queen Henttawi, showing the skin burst by the subcutaneous packing, Twenty-First Dynasty (from Elliot Smith, *Cairo Catalogue: Royal Mummies,* 1912).

Fig. 42. Queen Makare and her 'child', a female hamadryas baboon (from Elliot Smith, *Cairo Catalogue: Royal Mummies,* 1912).

experts, the Abd el-Rassoul brothers, who were then finally convicted. Thus the pharaohs who were described in the previous chapter came to rest in the present museum, providing a unique opportunity for us to gaze upon the features of those who lived and ruled thousands of years ago.

The reburials also provided the Twenty-First Dynasty restorers with the opportunity to observe the remains and they noticed that, although the New Kingdom methods were excellent, they had not resulted in a totally lifelike appearance, because of the desiccation of the corpses. A change in the technique of mummification therefore resulted, with packing being placed under the skin through various slits in the torso and limbs. The surface was then often painted, with artificial eyes inserted, so that a doll-like appearance was created. The packing materials were usually mixtures of linen, fat, soda and sawdust, and changes in these substances over time has caused some of the bodies to swell (to resemble Michelin men). The packing within Queen Henttawi's cheeks burst open, so her painted features are no longer attractive, although her head is adorned by an elaborate coiffure of twisted black string. At this stage, the viscera were wrapped around genii and re-inserted into the body cavity. Queen Henttawi's embalming wound was sealed with a gold embalming plate bearing the Eye of Horus. The body of the God's Wife of Amun, Makare, was also packed to stimulate the state of pregnancy, for she had died in childbirth. A small wrapped mummy in her coffin proved to be a female hamadryas baboon and not a child as was thought before it was X-rayed.

From the Third Intermediate Period (Twenty-Second Dynasty) the art of the embalmer rapidly declined. The viscera were placed in the body until the Twentieth Dynasty and then in parcels placed between the legs accompanied by dummy canopic jars. There was a revitalisation in tomb architecture and furbishment in the Twenty-Sixth Dynasty. By the Persian and Graeco-Roman periods, mummification had become democratised and was extended to a wider range of people. Mummies were often mishmashes with jumbled incomplete bodies made complete with bones, pottery or palm fibres. Inscribed wooden tags identified the bodies, which then could be stacked in communal tombs. The body beneath was covered with black resin like bitumen, from which comes the term 'mummy', Arabic for 'bitumenised thing'. Preservation was limited, and bodies (particularly those of women) had obviously been kept back from the embalmers, allowing time for maggots and beetles to attack, for these were often embedded in the resin. It must also have added to the gruesome nature of the job for the embalmers. More attention was paid to the external appearance, with elaborate bandaging forming diamond-shaped patterns with gilded studs in the centres, and there were cartonnage head, foot and breast pieces. The cartonnage head masks were frequently gilded and evolved into the wax encaustic mummy portraits painted on thin wooden panels and inserted into the bandages; it seems that the mummy was kept on show in the house before burial. As Christianity took over the land in the third and fourth centuries AD, the custom of mummification finally faded. Bodies were simply laid on boards in their clothes, but in the early Coptic period they were packed around with salt and vegetables, a remnant of the habits of the past.

Animal mummies

The practice of mummification was also applied to animals. These were rarely pets, but animals with the attributes of gods. Animal worship was an ancient custom; different creatures became the totems or fetishes of individual localities and, on the

Fig. 43. Twenty-Second to Twenty-Sixth Dynasty anthropoid coffin of Ta-menkh-Amen in the Museum of Victoria, Melbourne, Australia. (MOVX 79620. Courtesy of the Department of Anthropology and the Council of the Museum of Victoria, Australia).

unification of Egypt, some of the regional gods became national deities. Most gods and goddesses became anthropomorphised, retaining only their animal heads; others such as Ptah of Memphis and Amun of Thebes became fully human in form. Each god was connected with certain animal species which embodied their attributes. Therefore the Egyptians did not worship animals, but they kept the sacred creatures in captivity as divine representatives in association with the temples of the gods. The vogue which developed for the mummification of these animals coincided with the rise in popularity of the stone or bronze animal figures in the Saite Period (Twenty-Sixth Dynasty). These statues were left as votive offerings at local temples and the mummies may have been less expensive substitutes.

The first known animal mummies, and the last to survive, were those of the bulls associated with the cults of Apis at Memphis, Mnevis at Heliopolis and Buchis at Armant. The burial place of the Apis bulls at Saqqara is known as the Serapeum; the earliest burials took place in the New Kingdom, the last in late Roman times. It is a complex of underground galleries with vaults opening off them containing the huge granite sarcophagi of the bulls. Only one sacred bull, an animal with special markings, was kept in Memphis. When it died, it was mummified, attached with bronze clamps to a wooden board and left to rest in the Serapeum with a stela recording its date of death. The mothers of the Apis bulls were also buried in gallery vaults at Saqqara, and the mothers of the Buchis bulls in separate tombs like the bulls at Armant.

The temple of Nectanebo II of the Thirtieth Dynasty at Saqqara was dedicated to Isis, Mother of the Apis, and there were separate chapels for two underground cemeteries of other sacred animals. One was devoted to the baboons sacred to Thoth, of which over four hundred mummies survived, and the other to hundreds of thousands of falcon mummies. To the north and south of the temple of Nectanebo are more honeycombed galleries, which cut into earlier tomb shafts; these contain about half a million ibis mummies, a bird which was sacred to Thoth. Each baboon mummy was fixed into a wooden box with gypsum plaster and then closed into a recess with a limestone slab detailing the date of its burial. The birds were intricately wrapped in linen and then sealed in pottery jars, which were laid in rows in the galleries. There must have been intensive bird farms to satisfy the demand; it has been estimated that ten thousand birds per annum were interred at Saqqara.

Fig. 44. (Left) Roman mummy with elaborate studded bandaging and wax encaustic panel portrait of the deceased from Hawara.

Fig. 45. (Right) Wax encaustic portrait on a wooden panel of a lady wearing gold earrings and necklace, from Hawara, Roman period. (UC 30081).

Fig. 46. Bronze statuette of the sacred Apis bull wearing the sun disc and protective uraeus (UC 16462).

Ibises and baboons were also buried at Tuna el-Gebel, the necropolis of Hermopolis Magna, the city of Thoth. Ibises were also buried at Abydos, where there was a subterranean cemetery for the dogs associated with Khentiamentiu, a necropolis god there. Crocodiles, sacred to Sobek, were buried in the Fayum and at Kom Ombo, where their mummies can still be seen stored in the Graeco-Roman temple. The Nile perch was mummified at Latopolis, the ram at Mendes and Elephantine (where it was sacred to the creator god Khnum), and at Dendera there is a mixed cemetery containing birds, cats, gazelles, ichneumons and snakes.

One of the most popular cults of the late period was that of the cat, in honour of the goddess Bastet at Bubastis. Devotion became so fanatical that Diodorus Siculus, a Greek historian

Fig. 47. Bronze figure of a cat with kittens seated on a lotus flower (UC 8201).

visiting Egypt in the first century BC, saw a Roman lynched after he accidentally killed a cat. The cats were specially bred and had their necks broken for purchase and mummification for pilgrims. After evisceration and drying in natron, the forelegs were drawn down the body, the hind legs up against the pelvis, and the whole body was wrapped in linen, often elaborately decorated. The bronze cat with an earring, or Bastet with sistrum and basket — much sought after by collectors — and the cat mummy are particularly evocative relics of ancient Egyptian customs.

Other animals were mummified, some of which were not sacred, and some of the sacred animals such as lions do not seem to have been preserved. The decline in animal mummification coincided with that of human mummification as Christianity spread in the third century AD. One of the last entrenchments of ancient belief and practice was the persistence of the Apis worship until the Serapeum was destroyed in the fourth century after an edict of the Emperor Honorius banning sanctuaries for pagan use. The motivation behind the practice of mummification then passed into the realm of mystery and mumbo-jumbo until the ancient texts could once again be read in the nineteenth century. The evolution of archaeological methods during the early twentieth century and the application of scientific palaeopathological techniques up to the present day are still adding to our knowledge of how the Egyptians lived and died.

7
Modern studies and bibliography

Herodotus (fifth century BC)

A Greek historian who described the techniques of mummification used in Egypt. Three grades of treatment were available: 1: The brain was drawn from the nostrils with an iron hook and dissolving drugs; Ethiopian stone was used to incise the flank and the entrails were removed; the body was cleansed with palm wine, purified with incense, stuffed with perfumes and sewn up; it was soaked in natron for seventy days, washed and bandaged. 2: Cedar oil was injected into the anus, the body was soaked in natron, and the oil let out with the dissolved internal organs. 3: A purgative was used as a wash, and the body soaked in natron.

Lloyd, A. B. *Herodotus Book II, Commentary 1-98*. Leiden, Brill, 1976.

Pettigrew, Thomas Joseph (1791-1865)

A British surgeon who became interested in Egyptology after meeting Belzoni in 1818. The first modern scholar of the subject of mummification, he commonly gave public demonstrations of mummy unwrapping.

Pettigrew, T. J. *A History of Egyptian Mummies and an Account of the Worship and Embalming of Sacred Animals*. London, 1834.

Lortet, Louis Charles (1836-1909)

A French naturalist who prepared the Cairo catalogue of mummified animals found in Egypt.

Lortet, L. C. and Gaillard, C. *La fauna momifiée de l'ancienne Égypte*. 1903-9, Archives du Muséum d'Histoire Naturel de Lyon, IX-X.

Cairo Medical School (founded 1907)

Research on mummification was conducted by three professors:

Ruffer, Marc Armand (1869-1917)

English professor of Bacteriology. He pioneered methods of examining soft tissues, conducted experiments in mummification and identified diseases.

Ruffer, M. A. (editor Roy L. Moodie). *Studies in the Palaeopathology of Egypt.* Chicago, 1921.

Smith, Grafton Elliot (1871-1937)

Australian Professor of Anatomy from 1900 to 1909, afterwards at Manchester and then University College, London, 1919-36. He examined human remains from many sites, including the royal mummies in Cairo, and Tutankhamun. Proposer of the Diffusionist theory: Egypt as the source of most customs and beliefs.

Smith, G. Elliot, *A Contribution to the Study of Mummification in Ancient Egypt with special reference to the measures adopted during the Twenty-First Dynasty for moulding the form of the body.* 1906.

The Royal Mummies. Cairo Catalogue, 1912.

With Dawson, W. R. *Egyptian Mummies.* 1924.

Lucas, Alfred (1867-1945)

English Professor of Chemistry; later chemist to the Egyptian Antiquities Service, who analysed many materials and substances, conserved objects and experimented in mummification using pigeons, proving that dry natron, not a solution, was used; his pigeons are still mummified.

Lucas, A. *Preservative Materials Used by the Ancient Egyptians in Embalming.* 1912.

Ancient Egyptian Materials and Industries. 1926; revised by Harris, J. R. 1962.

Derry, Douglas E.

Anatomist and surgeon. Professor of Anatomy in the Faculty of Medicine, Egyptian University, who examined various mummies including those of Djoser and Setka, Amenophis I (by X-rays), 'Akhenaten' and Tutankhamun.

Various papers, particularly with Engelbach, R. 'Mummification' in *Annales du Service,* XLI, 1942, pages 233-65; and Appendix I in Carter, H. *The Tomb of Tutankhamun,* II, 1927, also Book Club Associates, 1972.

Chicago, USA (see also Michigan)

First comprehensive use of X-rays in the study of mummies.

Moodie, R. L. *Roentgenologic Studies of Egyptian and Peruvian Mummies.* 1931.

Gray, P. H. K. (died 1984)

A British doctor and radiologist; X-rayed 133 mummies in British and European collections during the 1960s; collaborated with various people including Warren Dawson (1888-1968), who had maintained an interest in the subject since his work with Elliot Smith.

With Dawson, W. R. *Catalogue of Egyptian Antiquities in the British Museum, I: Mummies and Human Remains.* 1968.

With Slow, Dorothy. 'Egyptian Mummies in the City of Liverpool Museums'. *Liverpool Bulletin Museums Number Volume 15.* 1968.

Sandison, A. T.

A pathologist based in Glasgow who studied disease, particularly through histological examination of ancient tissue in the 1960s.

'The Study of Mummified and Dried Human Tissues' in Brothwell, D. and Higgs, E. (editors), *Science in Archaeology.* Thames and Hudson, London, 1970.

Harrison, R. G.

An anatomist from Liverpool who restudied the remains of 'Akhenaten' and Tutankhamun with a view to establishing similarities.

Articles: 'An Anatomical Examination of the Pharaonic Remains Purported to be Akhenaten' in *Journal of Egyptian Archaeology,* published by the Egypt Exploration Society (for membership apply to 3 Doughty Mews, London WC1), volume 52, 1966.

With Connolly, R. C. and Abdalla, A. 'Kinship of Smenkhare and Tutankhamun Demonstrated Serologically' in *Nature,* 224, 1969, pages 325-6.

Manchester (see also Melbourne)

Margaret Murray officiated at the unwrapping of the mummies of two brothers from Rifeh; an Egyptological and anatomical report was produced.

Murray, M. A. *The Tomb of Two Brothers.* Manchester Museum Publications number 18, 1910: (Khnum Nakht and Nekht Amun).

Rosalie David led a team of experts from the University Medical School in the early 1970s in X-ray analysis of the collection. One Ptolemaic mummy of a girl was autopsied in 1978 and studied in detail, including the analyses of its parasites and bandages. Features restored on a model of her skull, and also those of the two brothers, by Neave. The project continues. Symposia held in Manchester, 1979 and 1984.

David, A. R. (editor). *Mysteries of the Mummies*. Book Club Associates, 1978.

The Manchester Mummy Project. Manchester University Press, 1979.

Michigan (Cairo)

X-ray examination of the royal mummies in Cairo undertaken under the direction of the University of Michigan School of Dentistry from 1966 to 1971, published in collaboration with the University of Chicago.

Popular account: Harris, J. E., and Weeks, K. R. *X-Raying the Pharaohs*. Macdonald, London, 1973.

Technical report: Harris, J. E. and Wente, E. F. (editors). *An X-Ray Atlas of the Royal Mummies*. University of Chicago Press, 1980. With sections by Zaki Iskander (techniques) and Kent Weeks (dentistry) and others; full bibliography.

Palaeopathology Association (USA/Canada)

Founded in 1973 by Aidan Cockburn. PUM II mummy from Pennsylvania University Museum, X-rayed and autopsied in 1973 in Detroit; resin analysed as oils of juniper and camphor and gum resin myrrh. PUM III and IV also autopsied.

ROM I, autopsy of Royal Ontario Museum mummy in Toronto, 1974, with the Detroit group of the Palaeopathology Association. Further mummies X-rayed at University of Pennsylvania in conjunction with an exhibition in 1980.

Cockburn, A. and E. *Mummies, Diseases and Ancient Cultures*. (abridged paperback edition), Cambridge University Press, 1983.

University Museum Handbook number 1: *The Egyptian Mummy: Secrets and Science*. Philadelphia, 1980.

Melbourne (Australia)

Museum of Victoria project of conservation of the mummy of Tjeby and his coffin from a Middle Kingdom tomb at Sheikh Farag begun in 1983. Dental pathology being studied; reconstruction of his head in wax by Mineur according to methods of Kollman and Büchly. As yet unpublished, information courtesy of Colin A. Hope, author of 'Tjeby the Elder from Sheikh Farag

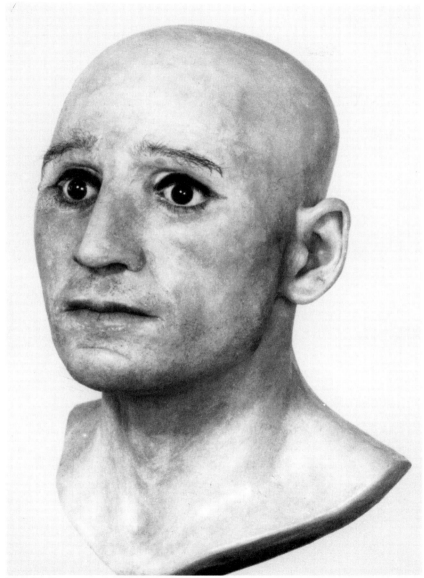

Fig. 48. Reconstruction of the head of Tjeby the Elder by Mineur from the Middle Kingdom Tomb 5105 at Sheikh Farag. (Courtesy of the Department of Anthropology and the Council of the Museum of Victoria, Australia.)

Tomb 5105' in *Abr Nahrain,* the Journal of the Department of Middle Eastern Studies, University of Melbourne, volume 22 (1984). He also presented a paper with Margaret Perkins at the Science in Egyptology Symposium held at the University of Manchester in June 1984. The proceedings of the Manchester Symposia (1979, 1984) will also contain reports on the latest British, American, European and Egyptian research into mummification and related topics.

General

Andrews, Carol. *Egyptian Mummies.* British Museum, 1984.
Hamilton-Paterson, J., and Andrews, Carol. *Mummies: Death and Life in Ancient Egypt.* British Museum and Collins, 1978.
Leca, Nage-Pierre. *The Cult of the Immortal.* Paladin, 1980.
Spencer, A. J. *Death in Ancient Egypt.* Penguin, 1982.

Fig. 49. (Opposite) Map of ancient Egypt, showing the principal archaeological sites.

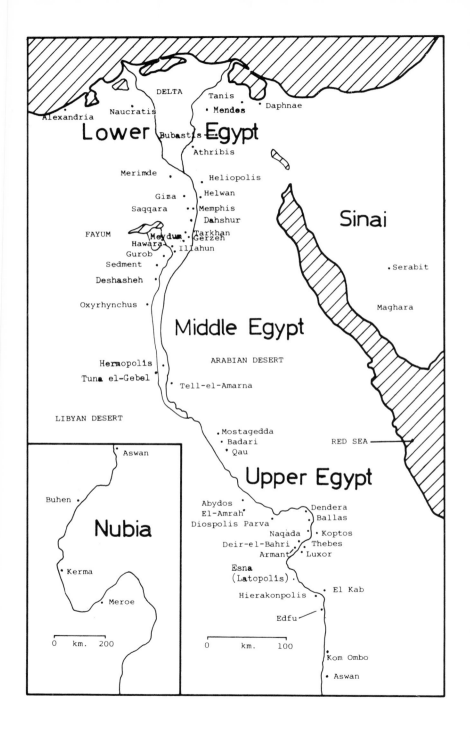

Acknowledgements

The people who most encouraged and helped my research into mummification were Don Brothwell, who was my superior in the Sub-Department of Anthropology, British Museum of Natural History (1964-5), and Eric Uphill, Research Fellow of the Department of Egyptology, University College, London, and Extra-Mural Lecturer. As examiners, he and Professor H. S. Smith set the topic in the special section of my Diploma in Archaeology final examination (1969). I would also like to thank John Rotheroe for inviting me to fulfil an ambition by writing this book, and Elizabeth Keyzar for moral support and typing.

Unless otherwise stated in the captions, all illustrations are copyright of the Department of Egyptology, University College, London. The drawings are by Stuart Munro-Hay. Acknowledgement is made to W. J. Murnane and Penguin Books Ltd for permission to reproduce the Chronology on pages 5 and 6.

Index